The Mottled Air

Poems by

Paul Christensen

Panther Creek Press
Spring, TX

Published by Panther Creek Press
SAN 253-8520
116 Tree Crest
P.O. Box 130233
Panther Creek Station
Spring, TX 77393-0233

Cover photo by the author
Cover design by Adam Murphy
The Woodlands, Texas
Printed and bound by Data Duplicators, Inc.
Houston, Texas

1 2 3 4 5 6 7 8 9 10

Library of Congress Cataloguing in Publication Data

Christensen, Paul

The mottled air

I. Author   II. Title   III. Poetry

ISBN 0-9718361-7-5

Acknowledgements

The following poems have been previously published, some in different versions from those printed here. The author wishes to thank the editors and publishers where they first appeared.

"Dining at Midnight," *The Onset Review* (Spring 1999): 6.

"A Poem without Blackbirds," "Un poema sin mirlos," *Terra Incognito* 2 (Winter 2001/2): 57.

"What the Citizens of Corpus . . . " *New Texas 91* (Denton, TX: U. of North Texas/ Center for Texas Writers, 1991); rpt. *Texas in Poetry: One Hundred Fifty Years.* Denton: U. of North Texas, 1994; rpt. in *Texas in Poet 2.* (Ft. Worth, TX: Texas Christian University Press, 2002); rpt. in *Places*Voices*Landscapes*Cultures*, ed. Jacqueline McLean and Leslie Ullman (Iowa City: U. of Iowa Press, 2003).

"Marriage," *Borderlands: Texas Poetry Review* 10 (Fall 1997): 30; rpt. *Best Texas Writing*, ed. Brian Clements (Dallas, TX: Firewheel Editions, 1999).

"The Motel," *Inheritance of Light,* ed. Ray Gonzalez. Denton, TX: U. of North Texas Press, 1996, p. 170.

"Driving Toward Houston," *Southwestern American Literature* (Spring 1998); rpt. *Ecotropic Works*, ed. John Campion (Berkeley, CA: Ecotropic Books, 1999); rpt. *Poetry in Texas 2.*

"Night Journey," *Gulf Stream* 12 (1997).

"The Horse," *Poetry Motel* 7 (Winter 1997); *In a Field of Words,* ed. Sybil Estess and Janet McCann (Upper Saddle River, NJ: Prentice Hall, 2003).

"The Navasot' Bottoms," "The Mist over Lake Somerville," "Texas in the Middle Nineteeth Century," "Doors," *In a Field of Words,* ed. Sybil Estess and Janet McCann (Upper Saddle River, NJ: Prentice Hall, 2003).

"A Prayer," *Odd Angles of Heaven*, ed. David Craig and Janet McCann (Wheaton, IL: Harold Shaw Publishers, 1994).

Table of Contents

This one's for Catherine, tried and true

THE MOTTLED AIR OF APRIL

The sun is a pulse on my arms.
Rain forecast for afternoon but for now
the sky is a civil war of swirling currents,
blowing in clouds from the Gulf,
parting the gloom with jags of cobalt
heaving with that dark body of light --
so fierce it showers down upon us
with scorching generosity, until we turn
away to cool ourselves.

Overhead a squalor of onrushing fields
of air bloated like bellies, tumbling
on the winds, while the bald head
of terrifying authority glares down
like a general in the midst of battle.
I read my thoughts in what I see,
my lunge for order having disintegrated
in a string of failed romances,
lost ambitions. I came up gasping for air
out of that mire of wronged emotions
grabbing hold of a slippery post
tilting in the waters of your sympathy.

I'm better now; compromised, but better.
A survivor of youth and middle age,
a soldier come home from the front
with his fingers and toes, a battered heart.
I sit out when it's not too hot, on
the white chair of a yard strewn with
dandelions and fists of weeds, accepting
what I am. I see myself in that ever-shifting
sky above me, going almost dark and
then, wrenched by the corkscrew air
of coming rain, burst into light again.

DINING AT MIDNIGHT

The dark is edible, a meal
of shadows and memory.
What soul is not famished?
What spirit can withstand
the ache of a vanished sound,
or smell, a door slamming forever?

The woods are dense columns
entering the sky, but in the dwindling
paths along the ground
go certain footsteps we pursue,
and are left gnawing on echoes.

Wait, I say, reaching for my first kiss.
But already it is gone, time yawning
in the space between us.
The room is crushed by a bulldozer,
earth falling through the windows.

My childhood bed, stuffed with dreaming,
floats in the dark underworld
among refrigerators and broken stoves,
the muffled singing of radios
and blind TVs. An old Ford
points its battered face toward oblivion.

Invisible nurture, coming to the mouth
as words, no taste on the tongue.
A closed eye, long, uneven breath
and we are done.

IMAGINARY TRAVELS THROUGH ARIZONA

the lights are on in the pueblo
the ladders drawn close
to the terraces, a sound
of wooden bowls being
turned deep in the kiva

the red earth glows
and drains its starlight
from the hills
the path of the sun
is lit by what vanishes

a drum sounds softly
where a hand has touched
the skin, and pushed
a fist of air through sleep

bodies stir, giving up
old fathers and the arms
that held them
when they fell
out of the named places
into the unnamed

let there be more
to morning than a groan
and two sighs, a rattle of spoons
as the mind awakes
and sloughs off its serpent skin

something must emerge
with the waking, a flowering
of amulets and tokens
spells cast by the breath of gods

carried into light
as if the world were heaven

RITES OF SPRING

A bouquet of mint and pomegranate flowers
waggles in a boy's fist. In love for the first time,
he tiptoes out of his skin, discarding
the sack of ignorance that was his home.
Goodbye all the toys, the eyeless bear,
an armless soldier heading off to war
under the couch, where the cat lurked.

It's the nudge under the heart, the knock
in the groin come spring, sap running
in the brain and slopping down into the heart,
causing a kind of drunkenness. He wobbles
where he goes, his arms too long
for the task ahead, holding of a waist
while his head dives into murky waters for a kiss.

Where he goes, spiders come with him,
a bird sails overhead in its bird path, undeterred.
Wind blows behind, fluttering his hair, and a
puff of smoke becomes a flock of butterflies.
The gardens are sodden with dew, and
all things fertile and awake crawl toward
their mates, blunt, wicked, and throbbing.

SUMMER OPERA AT THE CINCINNATI ZOO

When the soprano reached for maximum breath
to belt out a final aria before the cymbals crashed,
a hippo joined her in a lover's duet, and
the macaws made their choral overtures.
Ah, where's the python with his great coiled
body when we need him? What note could he
sound from his memories? That large, meandering
tube contains a pagan music long withheld while
La Traviata probed love's breaking heart.

The zoo keepers roamed a caged wilderness
of tapirs and pacing lions, a bull elephant swaying
on his two left feet, one fore pad wide as
a tympanum dragging in the dirt, while the *basso profundo*
reached down into his torso for a final note.

These were the days when opera found its summer
home inside the zoo, and ladies adorned in feathers
and silk rocked in their folding chairs.
Old men yawned and waited for the intermezzo,
or for anything to happen -- a lion leaping loose
to enter the scenario, his mane shaking as he walked
on stage, bellowing his contribution to the plot.

In that vital darkness throbbing with eyes
and panted breath, wild notes leapt gutturally
into naked air, hot with the rage at being
dragged from paradise to this iron ghetto
where humans mocked their rank despair.

EATING IN THE WOODS

A descent, steep enough to humble
the knees to crouching, hands out
on either side to slow fate.
Cool wind on the face, sounds
of water far off. The animals
come here to drink; their prints
are under me. Slow down, there's time.

When a goal matures into ledges,
be sure what you dreamed.
Your soul hungers, but so does the belly.
Is this enough, you ask, scaling the loose
surface, the drops and switchbacks
meant to dissuade the cowards,
meek stay-at-homes?

I go on; doubt is my enemy.
It grows old hedges and barriers,
hahas to trip the unwary strayer.
I have fallen enough to wear
my history darkly.
My eyes have an eagle's
look of anger, and hope.

This is the moisture pressing
inward, the softer earth
near one's faith. A strange hand
reaches out of green nothing
to feed me – offering the only food for miles –

eat the acorn, Indians did. It is not
as bitter as you think.

And what communion is this,
acorn melting on the tongue,
the sap of darkness running
over speech into the heart?

NEAR VULTURE PEAK

You reach with your eyes along each rim
of this slant-down canyon, groping with
insect fingers of light. And beyond, well
don't look too hard -- you'll find yourself
tumbling among the clouds of sunset,
not a star to mark your progress.

The path is a crunch of stone and dust,
your feet at home among the windflaws.
But where is your heart in all this rocky heave?
It longs for more, something beyond it all,
beyond even the tipped gold crags, the lone
bird's sliver of cries against the cliffs.

The path unravels, no foot print to reassure
you an answer lies beyond its final turn,
where the air rises out of a muttering
ribbon of water tracing the parched landscape,
like a thought roaming among a heap
of syllables, never to be spoken.

MEDITATION AT LICK CREEK

A pile of sticks and a creek of black water.
Is this all we are? A little flowing through
a woods, a turn where the mud bank
hangs together snarled in hackberry roots,
a fly hung over the air dancing in a mote
waiting for something -- anything. Maybe
that's an idea. Or a moment of affection,
come to this idle place, this still, and breathless
impasse fringed by pepper grass.

Somewhere, another pile of sticks.
Another you. A ribbon of lacy, sun-embroidered
mesh gulping at shadows, dissolving under
the heft of an old refrigerator, coming to
again in a second marriage illuminated
by minnows and pig prints. Ah this
theater of mauve bowers, where we perform
our roles, sung to by grackles
and weepy owls, tragic to the last starlight.

ROAD KILL

It could be the skunks knew something
when the cars killed them. Their postures
in the street, flattened but belly up,
paws still clawing at survival, have
their vigils kept by large, officious buzzards.
Something in the gray woods, the rolling
and cut-down fields, knows when it's time.
The small ground life comes shuffling
out of the overarching bushes, revealing
their striped bodies to the air, the hawks
swirling in confusion at so much fruit
moving toward their anxious maws.
But here we come, an onrush of certain
weight buttressed by chrome and tires,
a heaving bolt of fire belched in our iron
bodies, hurling out of nowhere, going
nowhere, caught in our own philosophical
oblivion, and now made more oblivious
by the cold soothing air, the murmurs
of a radio, as our speed devours them,
one by one, in a distant shock, a muffled
thump and we are gone again, the air
behind us wreathed in the tannic, onion-
bitter scent of someone else's death.

THE WHORES

They are drinking alone
on the outskirts of Manila,
around the abandoned naval base
at Subic Bay, whose arms of water
still inch forward under the burning land.

There, young men moved
like a centipede from the gray ships,
rippling in long coils from
under the wrapped muzzles of guns,
toward the narrow streets
hung with the blistered neon shields
of love.
                    The women were calm,
sitting in twos and threes
in bare rooms shattered
by jukeboxes. They drank the thin
whiskey of their momentary lovers
and laughed in all the clatter
of their business.

            But that is all history now,
the dark, volcanic land spreads
out from under their spiked heels
and the small brown feet
that poked up under the blond weight
of America, head home again.

LATE ONE TUESDAY NIGHT

I drive to the store for some cans of
tomatoes for dinner. The aisles are
empty, the kid sweeping doesn't look up
as I pass with my squeaking cart.
The butcher is through for the night,
hosing down the trays.

The apples shine like billiard balls;
the bananas are like marble ornaments,
the kind my mother used to dust
and heap up in a bowl of carnival glass
in the dining room. A woman picks up
an eggplant and puts it down again;
she looks around for pungent eggplants,
but there are none. She moves on,
showing no emotion.

Who will comfort us when the pure,
unblemished products of America
drive us crazy? Will there be voices
to guide us home from the mall
to a life made real again, in the
embrace of wounded vegetables, a
worm in our apple? Who will offer
us the spotted banana, so rich
in the sugar of its ripeness,
it will fill our lives with joy?

AFTER LOVE

My dreams are scattered along the river banks
south of here; I go down to inspect them
each time I talk to you. It wasn't love
or the despair that follows that made me
what I am; given the times we're in,
I'd say I have survived almost intact.
But I fail the assay test each time,
lacking the iron and silver necessary,
the rhodium that makes for character.
Once, you thought I was something
brighter than heaven, a burning knot
of phosphor, a dagger of platinum.
I am made of other elements, like those
flawed rocks you see tumbling down
from old volcanoes at Big Bend.
My heart is alive with crows, and
at night, when everyone's asleep,
I spread out my arms like two black clouds
and stand there, a small, tired moon,
thinking of you, thinking of nothing else.

BIG BEND NATIONAL PARK

That monstrous theater of eternity lies in ruins
where the road wanders, climbing out of
a gorge carved by Jurassic rages
to catch its breath in this Homeric underworld.

The sea floors of vanished seas still cling
like tattered gowns around the red-cored
towers of old volcanoes, ten million years
of fire having heaved and buckled land here.

What wonders to the eye, the mind numb
as a frozen bird caught in a winter blizzard.
The hand may touch these dusty fragments
of the Cretaceous era, the eye follow

the ghostly ribbons of Boquilla sediments,
but nothing explains the roar, the warfare,
the hell's gate rancor and tumult
of this land shaped by an angry god.

We stare like deaf mutes, and creep
among the brittle iron-ringing scree
under our sneakers, the wind so dry
it weathers our lips into stark silence.

A FAMILY HISTORY

My mother is dead; and now my father is laid beside her
in the Virginia earth, not twenty days ago, under the bronze
seal that says "Together Forever." They lie there,
one already turned to dust and a few bones,
the other plump and suited, wearing his socks
and clutching his last tie, his final memories of life.

In the ledge beside them is my brother's body, dead
these many decades, fallen among the cancer bodies
of NIH in Washington, a guinea pig of the government's
medical wards – pumped with every exotic in their
arsenal of experimental weapons, until shriveled down to
an envelope lumpy with joints and hip bones,
and a lopsided rib cage heaving with tumorous breaths.
Buried with an American flag presented by Marines
in crisp new uniforms, though he hated the military.

We were a family once, gathered under the diningroom
light to eat in silence, with winks and a few grimaces
over our plates while my father savagely ate his dinner.
My mother swung from a trapeze of blood sugar ropes
that lifted and dropped her down into chasms of despair,
and raised her again to a shrill satiric laughter.
We took turns doing the dishes while the TV muffled
its emptiness in canned applause and reruns.

Now there's only two of us alive, my older brother
living in his wooden house on Royal Street, dancing
on the tiny polished floor at Mulate's, his body
flying in all directions as the Cajun band rattled
the limits of its squeeze box and electric bass,
and banged blindly on the cymbals and snare.
And me, aging and fallen into a realm of offices
and sandwich lunches, still liberal after all these years.

IN THE DARK ROOM

My negatives hang like scrolls on the drying line.
This underworld of stacked windows, each with a ghost
in it, reversed from the living in their whiteness, their
howling mouths and black teeth, their hands fading
into a cascade of darkness from behind.

Among the stern gazes is my father's sleeping face,
a few days to live yet, taking his dreams sparingly
while the afternoon disintegrated.
He is casting last glances into corners of his mind,
remembering what shaped him, and made him lonely.

I leaned down into his bed and hovered
with my camera, peeling light from his body
and pasting it on my film, image by image,
his face floating on a river of sleep, barely
turning to survive the current's race for the sea.

These are my memories, his impotent emotions
reaching without hands or speech to embrace us,
recoiling at the first sign of our disbelief,
our skeptical hearts so used to his aloofness.
He was a rag sopping up what love he could

from his career, his vertiginous climb to
fulfillment, his lonely progress on the road
to happiness. Now he's among the shadows
I have captured and drained of blood,
their spectral patterns gazing out at me.

A POEM WITHOUT BLACKBIRDS

When animals dream, they ease
from their bodies like toothpaste.
Liberated from bone, they celebrate
being shadows – flowing under
doors, through fences – undoing daylight
until even their eyes disappear.

This is the air we sometimes hold
walking in the woods. Gray
in our palm, a dark thought
upon our shirt, something said
that thrills with a shrinking heart
from inexplicable grief.

And then it passes. We are strangers
under love, hardly speaking the same
language. My desires are like a foreign
city in which you fear to lose yourself,
so many dark, twisting alleys where
love would lead you, and leave you.

THE LOAN OF A HOUSE

The temptations lie everywhere,
the locked drawer, the bedroom closet,
a shelf out of reach in the kitchen.
What's in the cellar, under the spider webs?
In a corner of the attic, something
has held its breath for years, wrapped in tissue paper.
It lies there in a memory steep, a hole
in the raw nerves of time.

The chime in the downstairs hall
moans through the hours of afternoon
as you get used to your new body,
this framed house ticking at joist ends,
creaking on its cellar steps. The odor
so intimate as you part your way
stealthily through a drawer of sweaters,
it almost rises up to kiss your mouth.

In the enamel box an envelope
throbs with hurt, a straight pin
lodged in its own thin script, where
the dust of love falls freely from your hands.
You have levitated out of your stale
corner in Pittsburgh to this lush, green
avalanche of pains pouring from the attic,
swirling in motes as you pry open
this faceless stranger's lips
and probe each hidden word,
to feed your guilty, famished eyes.

A SO-CALLED LIFE

In the kingdom of lost desires, you are
only a tenant farmer eking out his pay
with a dust cloth and a sack of bills
to mail. House-sitter nonpareil,
professional loafer and legal squatter,
you take your shelter from want ads
pleading for someone to water the house
plants and let in the cats, and forward
the messages to a Caribbean address
for six weeks. Okay, okay, you pass
your interview with flying colors and
a borrowed blazer and tie. You're
the butler now, to an invisible master
and mistress, whose only chiffon trace
is the Persian cat sleeping belly-up
in a hairy shadow on the sofa. At night,
sometimes, a call comes in with a voice
furry with sleep, asking for someone
you do not know, and you reply
with undetectable hope the caller
might settle for less. A substitute, who
not only gorges on old ice cream pints
left in the freezer, but ransacks the pantry
for the last two tins of Vienna sausages
from which to scrabble up a supper.
You have a life, poured like sugar into
a shingled box, to be spooned
out each day in cat litter boxes and

the mail, that snow that drifts in by
the envelope and piles up in the corners
of the parson's table. Meanwhile, and
meanwhile is all there is, you mount
the stairs to the next story, and the next.

AT THE EZ PAWN IN AUSTIN

The pawn shop's adrift in afternoon light.
A shadow hangs like bankruptcy over
the jewelry cases, where a slender brown woman
eyes the diamond rings. Her kid is hanging by a finger
from her left hand, while her right clutches a wad
of bills. Her eyes are full of scrutiny, as the clerk
fans her luxurious purple nails in a soundless
tarantula dance. Night is mounting in the east,
moving toward us like a thunder storm.

But love is used to the dark, and thrives in this
arid landscape. A ring might cost fifty dollars
and she has forty. No angel descends out
of the humming tube lights to plead her cause.
She goes along, eyes like flashlights, over
the rings, each with a slightly smaller stone,
a tarnished and dimpled gold thin as wire
washed up on the shores of shipwrecked marriages.
The one she wants glitters like mica
and cold starlight, a bit of heaven.

She's lost among the velvet rows of light.
The stale air of abandoned televisions
rises into her imagination; she wanders
among failed guitars and hanged clarinets,
the drill presses idle beside the nail guns,
the heap of leather tool belts, and industrial
stilts for hanging ceilings. All that labor
and struggle just to stay alive, turning sour
at the first crack in the heart, ending
in this tomb of forgotten sorrows.
She stands between Hades and Eros
as iron curtains batten down the world.

AT HYÈRES, JUST BELOW TOULON

The moon half-buttoned in the sky
hangs nonchalantly overhead.
We are bathed in light from the swimming pool,
all emerald and shivering with wavelets.

A voice is lost in the plush of the dark,
and the tinkle of someone's drink
crashes to the dripping tiles. Life
at nine o'clock on a week end, at
the seashore, but not on it - near enough
to smell the salty wind, the popcorn
vulgarity of the air.

　　　　A Ferris wheel winds
its riders through the glare and tinny
music, draining the shrill cries of
the roller coaster in its upward rush
to the sky, and the soft, dizzying heave
of bodies rounding the crest,
floating down again into blossoming
street lights, and that plain, predictable
world where we spend our lives.

ADMIRING YOUR HANDS

A scar on your hand
tells me the soul
of the tree that died
entered you.
Its branches rise
and follow the veins
of your tender skin.

May I kiss the place?
I smell soap, I smell
labor and love, humble
ways of living.

The hand is as light
as a leaf, and the scar
now blue, now silver
against the fan
of small blue veins
is a landscape of gods.

This is the miniature
Navajo sand map
of the soul's aspiring.
A tree on a broad plain
with blue leaves
and the mellow sun rising
in the glow of your skin,
the fruitfulness of your hands

that have broken beans
and kneaded dough, and stirred
and offered, and accepted

this cicatrix as the bud
accepts the rose.

WHAT THE CITIZENS OF CORPUS, ROCKPORT, PALACIOS OR BRYAN NEED

What the citizens of Corpus, Rockport, Palacios,
        or Bryan need is
not a new tiller, or a pair of radials, a
        goose-neck trailer to pull

the yearlings into market, or tubs of loam to
        green up the bushes
along the drive. What they need least is that
        dish revolving in the yard,
up on its steel leg with a face lonely as abandoned children,
        looking for some satellite to hug,
to suck up love beams in its empty bowl
        and pipe them to a house of anxious
tempers and fried fish, and the wonder bread
        heaped up on a dinner plate.

What they need can't be bought or traded for a
        pair of Red Wings,
or settled out of court. It lies there like a veil
        of ice high up in the winter
twilight, the ghostly whisper of a
        phantom jet streaking its way
toward San Antonio. You can almost spell
        the letters out of sheer and stubborn
emptiness as he wings it
        over the colors of divorce
and sickness of heart -- the great way stations
        of the living.

What they need is not looped or dangled, or
       run up into the attic after Christmas,
or piled up along the back side of
       the house, where the mosses grow
and the roach settles for a nest.

       Need here is complicated by weather
and the slip and slide of dreams; things
       are tuned up like banjo strings
that the kids get to, untwist the pegs
       and let a clang of discord
run riot over the adult hangovers
       that greet the rising sun
each painful morning.

       It wouldn't take a psychologist
or a social scientist long to decipher
       the meaning of each town's main street;
those boarded store fronts
       and clean curbs, those long asphalt
corridors leading nowhere, or the woman
       who pinches her blinds to see whose
car warms up at the widow neighbor's
       drive. All those frozen lawns
with houses camped on them;
       a little smoke dribbling from chimneys,
buttery light in the living room windows,
       the sleep-heavy second stories
where love rots away in bed frames
       and darkened bathrooms.

God knows Maggie needs it, and poor Tom
    can't pitch the hay much
longer without it; and Bob writes bad checks
    with a stomach ache
worrying so hard; and Madeline allows herself
    no more indiscretions
with the delivery man; and Ralph knows
    his arteries are too small to
pump hope out of a dry well. And all lay
    sleeping this way and that,
half-slit eyes and burned out consciousness,
    waiting for the gentle drops of mercy
on their roofs, into their parched souls.
    What they all need glitters on the mouth,
and shags around like bears
    in the sleepy world of dying passions.

MARRIAGE

Near Quito, my mother once told me,
two windows peer out over the equator.
In one are flowers, iris and jonquil,
the long hungry throat of tiger lily lapping sunlight.
In the other, the stalks stand leafless.
One window gazes on summer, the other
on winter twilight. Ten feet separate these
squares of world, hung upon
grass pins and flocked with clouds.
One could almost stretch and touch them both,
and come apart along a line
drawn between desire and forgetting.
They're out of reach, not even
fingers can graze the membrane
of opposing worlds.

Instead, one looks, and moves about
in the uncertainty Keats described.
To deny one window or the other
reaches after power, and the mind closes.
There you are, passing in summer,
while I turn my back, looking
down into the blue condensing moment
of winter, the opal nut of ice lying
so close to what we think we love.

DRIVING HOME FROM AUSTIN

Our thoughts go dry
at the wild, uneven twist
of river flats, corn-green

and nubbed with cotton
in undulating wales,
fields spired with derricks

and gin sheds, tin silos
tarnished to watery glare,
the unmoved immensity.

Who can stay human under
the unbending weather?
Under these grating heavens

and warped earth?
Only a strong god rules
the wayward spirit,

and breaks its soul
in bone-haunted corners
of the Brazos prairies.

Tunis, then Clay, Mumford and
Independence, the way drags
its history forward

on thin skeins
laced with thorn,
spiked berry,

dumb-struck buzzards
floating in thermals
over a smudge of road kill.

The air coils upward
into yellow sky, leaving
the ancient grass

brimming with silence.
The ground is old,
wrinkled and shoved among

rusting implements, a tractor
on its side, hulked
like dragon bones

against the coiled wire
on wooden drums.
Night advancing

in pools of shadow,
first windows, then
barn, work shed,

animals in trances at cattle
guards, day holding
its breath as light

weakens into gold.
Somewhere the Brazos turns
a slow thrust

of mud and heat, borne
by soggy currents
further east, moist tempo

of decay, slow pulse
among the stagnant monuments,
eternal clay.

THE MOTEL

is a form against
    the land,
        moving toward us

its fragile outline
    crumbles in the
        long shadows of sunset

there are others
    who have drifted
        to its shelter

and lie wakeful and restive
    in the beds,
        waiting in the dark

as we approach the
    emptiness in which it
        takes its life

exhausted, our eyes pressed
    inward from the monotonous
        journey south

eager to sleep, to push
    away the limits of thinking
        and surrender

to awake in another country
   under the soft night
      where love is possible

and our small sins
   sit bold upon our skin
      like ancient charms

THE WHEEL

A wagon wheel is the mandala
of parched ground.
It lies abandoned among
fence posts and weeds, bone-
colored and wind-varnished.
It turned once under the groans
of a wagon loaded with grain
bound for the rutted hills of Eden.

It broke against silence
and was pulled from use, given
to the weather. It was a doorstep
to a palace of birds,
a boundary of ant kingdoms.
It's hub was a pocket full of wasps,
while its rim, removed by small green hands,
rolled toward the moon.

                        Now
it concedes roundness
to the leveling earth, and slides
gracefully under the vines
like a word forgotten among
old languages.

SUMMER NIGHTS

Where the tracks sidewind through
tall grass, among the tumbledown shacks
of the Brazos bottoms, the boys
stand around keeping the moon company,
bottle in hand, swapping tall tales
and curses until the girls go dancing.

As the stark white houses rot in silence
with their lonely beds, heat
thick in the parlors, old men
sleeping in their Lazy Boy loungers
before the muttering TV, the farm wives
play Bingo in the gymnasium.

The lights hum in the dance hall
and the smells of sugar and sweat
mingle in the breath. An arm
tenses at the feel of skin
in its bony hand, and a softness
wild as the sea gives in to love.

TORTILLA MOON

Dark *latino* skies scented
with lime water and salsa,
a boom box pounding the heart
in a cruising low-rider.
On the edge of town, money
moves from hand to hand
as night edges toward visions.

My *señorita*, my bruised
orchid in sweater and heels,
pushes me backward
under the trumpet flashes,
where the air is stained
with beer and lipstick.

Mi destino es su destino,
with the gold dangling
from your ears, and the mouth
electric with laughter.
Have you touched the beast
in my shirt? Or will
you coax it out with moans
and a rattle of ice cubes?

Corazon, corazon, the men
moving in a wave of neon shirts,
their bodies invisible beneath
their tooled and sparkling belts.
Each is in love with sorrow,
while the earth swings
on wide hips, sliding her low-heeled shoes
into the tangle of boots.

Let the cops dive beneath
our glitter; their fins leave
behind a silver wake, a shiver
of cold metal that grips the pulse
like handcuffs where they wait.
Someone is watching us,
we must be beautiful tonight.

THE CROW'S BRAIN

There is no exile, only blackness.
The tree shakes with glory,
the ground is a robe of wheaten plainness
jeweled with rain drops. A road leads
only to the treasure of fallen nuts;
the rind of some delicious secret
curls in the waterfall of sunlight.

Under every rock glows the worm,
moist pleasure tucked
in its divot of loam. When spring
comes on its ten-mile feet
into the roundness of earth,
one must beat the clouds with one's wings
and salute death with cawing.

DRIVING TO HOUSTON

The miles are more like time than anything --
disks of prairie turning
like clocks in either window

in each of them a cow stands
or a horse nods itself to sleep
a house darkens against the distance

We are the present moment, tangible as
breeze but no more, shifting the boundary
between East and West, this crumbling wall

of North behind us, sealing as we move
into the dissolving South, its unmade history
gushing like springs before us

2.

But to look at one's hands in this motion
is to be reminded of the dead eye
of time, its inert paradise of waiting

while the edge rips against the trade winds
and scrapes the boundary of air
littered with satellites

my hand in the dust of the windshield
against the dashboard's immobility of knobs
and the silent radio, potential as words

with the day splitting open
falling away in giant halves
of choice, neither way taken

only the forward cut, the planed light
peeling over the car and rolling behind us
like nudes in a water fall

3.

If only it were possible to get down
and leave the moment to itself, to drive
home without me

I could be satisfied to enter
the grass on either side,
the unfamiliar density of blades and pebbles

an abstract, alzheimered world
of shacks and rutted paths, the salt lick
half gone against an old bath tub

what will it give me if I lie down
arms outstretched, my heart aching
for a welcome, some sign

that what's estranged is alive,
enduring in our absence, still fertile
under the insulted wastes

NEAR CUT AND SHOOT

A tree near Cut and Shoot
is a fist raised to heaven,
with a cloud in its grip,
a wind wrapped around its arm.

Near Cut and Shoot the women
are sneaky as cats, roaming
the evening with
hunger in their eyes.

At Cut and Shoot, when the bar
turns off its sign, and the window
is bare as winter light,
the men think only of death.

Stretching out across the
sandy earth to the sea
are pine stands, straight
and thin as a beard's bristles,

and in them lie secrets
of how to live, how best to rise
and take life in the arms,
and kiss its lonely mouth.

How to believe once more
in the old ways, the fertile
gifts that were earth's bounty.
Some things remember, humble creatures

without eyes or minds.
A little knowledge of roots,
a speck of remembering
the seeds, the wild tea,

the sweetness of carrot leaf
and yaupon, the green magic
of Eden held in a tree's
shadow near Cut and Shoot.

NIGHT JOURNEY

Give me a bed roll
and some sandwiches
and I will go down
into the cold woods
for the night.

No flashlight or matches,
no tent to smother
out the wind and stars,
no watch or towel
or cap or ear muffs,
just what I have
and the blanket, some
food in the evening.

I will sit against
a sassafras tree,
if one grows there,
and rub the leaf
under my nose, and dig
the cold norther
as it comes down
over the tree tops.

If you are quiet
and unprepared, left
at the border of the wild
and the human,
the mild dark of forest
will begin to speak in small rivulets
of air. You will feel
the breath of the ground
lifting you, and the whole
tilting forest of wind create
a body around you.

THE HORSE

An old woman studies the mind
of a horse. Her window looks out
on the gray pasture, the black
horse standing in the morning's dazzle.

She imagines the horse
under her, her legs feeling
the body's response to earth,
a heft sliding easily from joint
to joint as they edge
toward the uncertain world.

To be ninety is to be held
by weak strings
to the heat of the sun.
One moves in a glass firmness,
at the limit of breaking.

THE NAVASOT' BOTTOMS

Follow a coon's tracks
through the razor grass,
cane, thistle weed, and whatever
thorn the summer is growing
to a scrub oak leaning
its scrawly legs over the river.
Bless yourself three times
and give thanks to the maker
of these muddy banks,
for beyond them lie ruins
of cotton fields and a rimless
earth of smoldering prairie.

Inside every pain is an Eden
pooled like glitter, waiting
to be found. Fish slide,
and the worm balances
on a leaf's edge, a wind
plays among the fine hairs
of a spider's legs. Soft things
move in and out of plush
mosses, and the pebbles
are gleaming gems in the lace
of the water. Kneel and
be thankful the earth
pays no attention to us.

THE MIST OVER LAKE SOMERVILLE

Morning comes over the roofs
in a flood of gold paint
and old suitcases full of shirts.
The whores are sleeping until noon
and will not know the gaudy
splendor of another Sunday.

They roll in dreams of money
and a beige Cadillac
heading south; they hear
the music of tuxedo players
sliding their trombones
into a cloud of silk.

The Christians are eating breakfast
to the mumble of radios,
carving a brick of margarine
to soften their toast.
Their shoes are hard, the soap
smells of troubled memories.

What the preacher does
is private knowledge; only
a certain devotee of holiness
can know the truth. He putters
at his mirror in a naked trance
touching the hairs of his mole.

Meanwhile, at the water's edge,
an egret draws in her wings
to plume herself in a crook
of cypress. It is a soul
caught in the clutches
of the flesh, white and unused.

TEXAS IN THE MIDDLE NINETEENTH CENTURY

We are faced with a small god
wrapped in Bible paper,
newly torn from the earth.
It wears a swaddle of roots
and mud, the red of a goat's blood
tinging its muscles.

The Indians concede its capture
and leave, vowing a return.
But under these fierce
heavens of an August noon,
we are the conquerors, and this
brown god of thorns and snake teeth

grows tame with our milk,
and sleeps in the crook
of our long sleeves. We move
in a procession of land-grabbing
and slaughter, driving the wildness
into heaven, easing the rivers
down a shallow grave of cotton fields.

Soon enough will rise our churches,
and a steeple to scrape
the stars and pierce the dark
with our ambitions. Already
the coyote weeps on a hill,
and hears the creep of human shoes.

With this lord of snaggle teeth
and profit, this god of double
chin, a belly full of gold,
this icon of oil gluts,
old demon-haunted plaster doll,
we shall not want for rage.

DOORS

There are doors that are always locked.
One never bothers to try them;
they have sealed themselves to the jambs
and are thicker than the walls, harder
than the house they guard.

Many have wept against them, their bloodied
fists trembling after the last knock.
Behind them are the last survivors,
giving up in the mirror
with a razor blade or bottle of pills,

as the living stand on the other side
with a cry buried in their throats.
Doors have a will larger
than the trees they come from, harder
than the screws that bind them.

The locksmith is their guardian
and sets the tumblers with a heartless logic.
The door will not live until the lock
goes in, and not rest until
the key is turned in it.

Then, with quiet rigor and devotion,
the door seals another passage
to the world. The house goes dark,
a light ebbs beneath the crack, a sign
of withering and fright, the mark of doom.

A PRAYER

I'm out there somewhere, wandering around
under the street lights. I can hear my own
footsteps coming through the wall.
It is raining out; the cars are like
griddle plates frying some mysterious
supper of birds and moon light.
Men are gathered at the counter reading
the Bible, smoking cigarettes. The coffee
is hot and sour, and leaves a rank
smell of burning leaves on their breath.

My loneliness rises like the winter sun,
and there are paths frozen
under the morning ice. No one is looking
for me. I am sealed behind the landscape,
in a corner of daylight where nothing
is possible. Soul-like and silent
as time, I wait, leaning on the shadow
of God, which has built up a pillow of
grit and dust in the mind. This is the
stranger who lurks in me, whom I reach
out to like a desperate child, begging
to be answered by this prayer.

Answer me, answer the door, any door, let
him in and call me when he comes. He's
wearing a blue shirt and thrift-store shoes,
he's out of touch. What you offer you give
to yourself. But you knew that. You knew
all along this was the word aching to
touch your tongue, to ride the nerves
out of your own darkness into love.

ONE FINE MORNING IN SAIGON
for Jane Flowers

This was the city that gave me
my first wife. Her small, lumpy
body was more primal than a
paleolithic Venus. Her mouth
was just another painted cave.

She threw her power forward
until I buckled and rolled headless
toward her. She used my body
like a stick, flopping me
wildly in her strangling grip.

In the foot of sunlight marking
her domain, the warm jungle
gathered at her feet, prying
up the tile, the cement
of the school room, opening

the crack of her terrifying tongue
when I went limping home.
Dear beaked and feathered girl,
my loving friend, whose hands
were as rough as talons

and tore the envelope of skin
hiding my cowering heart.
You gave me my first lesson
in war, loving me with
fierceness until you won.

THE MECHANICS OF FREEZING

At a certain point
of afternoon, you look up
and your body is silver
you are no longer young
the glass jar is filled
with an indefinable fragrance
of time, and wind, and memories
with your face in it, smiling back
from a great distance
forgiving what you are

if the phone should ring
don't answer it
sit a while, think of a meaning
to all this magic
in the world,
the power of change itself
and how your light feet
and poor kite bones
are capable of moon drift
and disappearances

It is time for a lover
someone new to enter your life
to take off your clothes
and settle you against
a cool wall, with the light
entering you from all sides
whose white shape you have
never known before
coming toward you with
a creak of leaves and twigs
and the fall weather
tight against your breathless
wonder and excitement

OBSCURE ACCIDENTS

Someone has run over the black dog.
It lies dead on the median strip,
black fur rippling in the wind.
The bridge rolls on forever
over the silent highway,
and children seem never to grow up.
They call out from behind the fence
and slowly, with broken joints,
the dog struggles to live again.

In the gray fields cows move
with elegant slowness toward the barn.
Night folds its clouds, and
the stars are like jagged shards
of glass. All is breathless before
the dying sun. In the purple twilight
only the houses survive, anchored
by light in every window.

A DIFFICULT WOMAN

The dress she wore was light as clouds,
and all her bones were like a peak.
Her spirit was as pure and free
as the wild ponies of Ocracoke.
She loved me with her angry arms,
and made me weep.

Silence was the gift she gave,
the round dark well of woman's love,
I drank from it and tried to speak,
but nothing came to break her spell.

> *Love is a thorn*
> *that cuts my lip.*

And on and on our days burned bright,
with rage and bitterness, and tears.
She tore my clothes, and ripped my books
and cursed me with her cold dead looks.
And on we loved like thrashing sharks,
and drank the blood our wounds gushed forth.

> *O love is like a briar bush*
> *that cuts my skin until I cry.*

Meek forgiveness I would beg, on knees
that trembled with my love.
Kiss these withered, hopeless lips
and give me cause to live my life.

I hope you die! was her reply,
and took the kitchen knife to bed.

The moon was like a sickle now,
shaving the stars down to their nubs,
clearing the dreaming night ahead
of all my hopes of having love.
Leave her at once, my mother said,
she has destroyed your livelihood.

O why is love so difficult
it carves my flesh away from bone.

She sleeps alone now in her bed,
her laughter creeping out of dreams.
She will not let me kiss her hand
or touch the face I love so well.

O teach me how to reach my wife
she stands before me like the Earth.

THE LAUGHING WOMAN

Laughter in another room.
We are dining below, trying
to eat, but the concentration
is gone. The laugh is strung out,
partly echoed by high ceilings.
Who could find the absurd
so easily, I wonder.
For us, the square room
boiled in yellow light,
rumbling with eating, is
no balm to an evening
in a strange city.

She is finished, the love making
over. Who left by the narrow
stairs remains a question.
She comes into the dining room
seriously, ready to eat.
The waiter is an old friend
and returns with the first
glass of thin red wine.
What does she know that
makes her laugh until her
ribs could break?

Now the last man tramps
heavily from the lobby
and the night clerk
begins the audit under
a green lampshade.
There is a woman, thin,
angry, who stands outside
the door smoking, looking
up and down the empty street
for strangers, anyone
to keep her laughing.

ABOVE THE WEISSENSEE AT OBERNAGGL
for Adi and Irene Wimmer

Past all the problems, all the doubts,
the road lifts you above the dense
pine and larch forest onto an edge
of brightness, with the blue lake
meandering below you.

You wonder what the shouting was about.
Why you couldn't just forgive and
go on, instead of crashing uphill
into whip-crack branches, the webs
veiling your eyesight, the heart
sobbing aloud in your twisted thoughts.

Ah the lake, rimmed by a limestone
shore turning the water into milky jade,
the deeper parts glowing turquoise with cold.
There is the clarity you couldn't have
before; the rocks visible on the rutted
lakebed, the fish hanging as if by
dreams in their watery chambers,
the sky above remote and archaic with
all its signs and patterns.

Believe in something, in this blue length
beside you, this curving affectionate
word filling an old glacial scar.

THE WAVE

On the birth of Aphrodite

Chronos crept up behind his father
with his honed sickle,
the wind stirring in the olive grove.

It was time; the ash bole
had grown thick, its leaves
folding outward in a canopy

darkening the ground below.
The tree reached heavenward
and challenged the sun.

A rush, sandals twisting in the earth,
the startled look, muscles
tensed, in-flexing, as blood

spread across his snowy gown.
The old gods fall, new ones make
passage to their place.

And out of heaven hurtled
the lost orbs of Uranus's groin,
flung seed, dropping heavily

to the loose, gray Aegean.

ii

The crash plowed the sea, carving
it with waves. The first
curled upward, frothy and light

as a flock of doves, pure as
the green fringe of spring,
the ground hushed and waiting

as a goddess formed, riding a wave
that swelled to shore.
Aphrodite, hair blown back,

her cloak falling open to
sea-flecked thighs, legs rose-
hued as pearls, closing

their coral shoals in tufts
of moss, breasts full, round
as the moon on sea-washed rocks.

iii

Cypress welcomes the gift, builds
a temple on a hill where love
adorns itself in rain and flowers.

The dark push of desire
brings Aphrodite into light,
her hand encouraging each seed

to plummet to the aching earth.
She moves on silent paths
of blood, entering each womb

in a tide of longings,
the nibbling lip of water
from the primal wave.

Each girl gives up her innocence,
her face like a paper lantern
lit by selfishness,

turns toward night,
rising to womanly perfection
before her startled father's eyes --

shielding the goddess with her
flesh, moving toward love
as every woman must.

A VISIT TO MY GRANDSON, SWAN

The cat, grubby with scars and a tick
over his right ear, comes slinking home
from another love battle, exhausted,
happy to find shade and
make his own rolled shadow.

A pram sits in the green grass,
in the cool of a plane tree,
the baby spread out in dreamless sleep,
with the love birds twittering
and griping in a cage above him.

A few chairs, a table with a shiny tea kettle,
some glasses for mint tea in this heat,
the time passing with ease
as we sit in silence, looking around
in a pause of our wandering talk.

An old two-seater plane flies
over us from the nearby aviation club,
its motor rasping in that cooked sky above us.
A cold bottle of *Veuve Cliquot* arrives
to toast the news of someone else's pregnancy.

UNDER THE CROW'S WING
Provence

The village sits out on a spit
of rocky earth, gnarled
like an old woman's fingers,
roofs tangled in a red blur
of tiles, pushing their tattered
eaves against the sky.

       The reviled
end of speech is woven in
a blue silence, words
creeping with long shadows
from the mouth, strung with
lights in each syllable's window
where muffled shouts end
splintered like a dish.

       They are leaving it all behind, that is
what you hear in the market.
Farms close, reopen as hotels
on the sleeping lap of earth,
the gods set free to loaf
in empty air, over the idle ground.

       A naked bulb hangs
like a criminal from
the ceiling, as something stirs, something
useless at the heart of words.

BRETON BULL

An idea moves gradually through him
that he's tired, and after a glacial rumination,
his knees go soft and parts of him lower
down heavily into the cool, moist sod.
His back rolls halfway to the side, and out
goes a leg, and his beautiful black balls
lie there on his thigh like egg plants.
He never left the fold, or cut the strings
to silence and participation. He belongs
to the worms and the ants beneath him.

This is where the Celts came screeching
to a halt, crossing the whole continent
to reach this soaked and limestone shelf
fading out into the churning sea. They
rolled stones in rows, and worshiped
the gods of iron and water, and heaved
the big boulders into altars on the lee
of the hills. Then they sailed further west,
looking until their hearts broke against
the shores of Scotland. They were done,
finished with the road, ready to believe
in a hanged god tied to his wooden cross.

The bull survived, walked behind them
on their lonely journey, and when they
were gone, he ate his grass, and observed
the silvery drift of the night sky, and felt

the cool black breeze before dawn.
He's free of all that desperation that
broke its hands chiseling dreams;
he built nothing in his entire history.
He has no history, and would deny it
if one were given to him. He believes in
the power of spring to arouse him into
rages of lust, and the rest of the time
he empties his mind by eating, and by looking.

ON THE ROAD TO LUCCA
for Signe

Here's a town bolted to a mountain,
hanging over a chasm of blue air
as if it were the last human door
before hell. Here and there, gouts
of geranium gashed between slats of iron,
a pink tongue climbing out of a jar,
clinging by green nails to an overhanging shutter.

What does love deliver in those
aching rooms? A night creaking on
breath's hinges, the moon unlaced
in the overhanging clouds, rain
half-suspended until it unclenches
all its mercy against the roof,
flooding those cavernous reaches
where our dreams unfold impossible desires.

Someone's eyes follow my transient blur
through the knotted curves of
descent, the white shutters falling open
for the evening's first breeze.
Someone yawns, stretches, hands
on her lower back, feet bare to the
marble floor, rooted, unchanging,
eternal against the fleeting reality
I plunge through, looking for experience.

FANTASIES AT FOUR O'CLOCK

Around three o'clock, or is it four?
I stare off into the emptiness above my desk
and a glass of wine appears,
staining the gray light with redness.
I bring it to my mouth
and the cold, spring sunlight
of another country spreads
into my thoughts. I am walking
in some unknown square, under
a clock tower's stone prominence,
with a woman in black dress observing me.

I throw my weary self into a chair
on the cafe terrace, and order
my first wine of the day. It comes
to my hand, and there it is again,
the compassionate and easing light
mixed with the dead, the amber
hue of forgotten summers, all that
glitter and scent of bones and smoke
entering me, filling my hollows
like a graveyard.

I am drifting over the tiled roofs
of a village, accompanied by swifts
and magpies, and the flutters of a faded
French flag beating the wind over
the post office. I am there,
not here in this gathering darkness
of an office high up in the air
overlooking the city of oblivion.